Lisa H. Calle's

DIVIDE and design

The American Quilter's Society or AQS is dedicated to quilting excellence. AQS promotes the triumphs of today's quilter, while remaining dedicated to the quilting tradition. We believe in the promotion of this art and craft through AQS Publishing and AQS QuiltWeek®.

Content Editor: Caitlin Ridings
Graphic Design: Chris Gilbert
Cover Design/Production Manager: Sarah Bozone
Director of Publications: Kimberly Holland Tetrev

Additional copies of this book may be ordered from the American Quilter's Society, PO Box 3290, Paducah, KY 42002-3290, or online at www.ShopAQS.com.

Library of Congress Cataloging-in-Publication Data

Title: Lisa H. Calle's divide & design / by Lisa H. Calle.
Other titles: Lisa H. Calle's divide and design | Divide & design
Description: Paducah, KY : American Quilter's Society, 2016.
Identifiers: LCCN 2016032024 (print) | LCCN 2016033020 (ebook) | ISBN
9781604603996 (pbk.) | ISBN 9781604603248 (e-book)
Subjects: LCSH: Patchwork--Patterns. | Quilting--Patterns.
Classification: LCC TT835 .C355 2016 (print) | LCC TT835 (ebook) | DDC
746.46--dc23
LC record available at https://lccn.loc.gov/2016032024

Dedication and Appreciation

My Husband, Jon, has always been my biggest fan throughout my quilting journey. I could not have done this without the support of him and my 3 wonderful boys, Brandon, Noah and Brody. Thank you! I love you!

Contents

Introduction

I first started machine quilting in 2004 and quickly realized that I had a passion for it. Having finished over 2000 tops for 300+ customers gave me a lot of time to practice. Like you, I had numerous machine quilters that I wanted to quilt like. You can look at my work and see how it has progressed over time to where I am now. I have my own style of quilting and this is what you should strive for; you will take bits and pieces of things you learn from all the teachers you have and come up with something that is unique to you.

Over the 10 years of customers quilting there have been some tops that have really stumped me. From a special quilt for a wedding, a quilt that had a lot of open space, or a quilt that I had quilted numerous times in the past. I found that I would resort to a widely used method of "standing and staring" until something magically popped into my mind. This definitely was not a productive use of my time as it took that magical pop quite a bit of time to arrive in my head. I decided it was time to be more efficient, so I would take a picture of the quilt and doodle on it till I got something I liked.

Playing Hookie was one of the first quilts that I used this method on. It wasn't that I didn't know what to put on it. I immediately thought of feathered wreaths, but wait, I wanted something unique. If I thought of feathered wreaths then probably others would too and so the process started. The process has evolved over time into what I am going to teach you in the coming pages.

As you start on your journey through this book, I want you to stretch yourself creatively. Don't go with the first design you sketch, do a couple, and see what you come up with. Try not to think about how you are going to execute it. I find if I like the design enough, I will find a way to make it happen.

The patterns that I've designed for this book are relatively easy and small. I find that it is nice to start small and actually finish the project than try and tackle a large project with a new technique.

Please send me pictures of your projects as I love to see what you all create!

The Process

We have all been there. Standing and staring at a quilt top thinking "What in the world am I going to quilt on this top?" While the stand and stare method is used quite often, it is not very effective. You will be amazed at the one of a kind works of art you can create using the ***Divide and Design Technique***, whether you quilt on a longarm, home sewing machine, or are a hand quilter. The method is divided up into three parts, dividing lines, design work, and fill work. Depending on the density of quilting you like, you may stop after any one of the parts.

Step 1: Black/White Picture

The first step is to take a picture of your quilt and print it off in black and white. By printing your quilt off in black and white you will see the true values of the colors in the quilt. You will be able to see which fabrics are truly dominant. By hanging the quilt so that it is flat on a wall you will get a more useful picture. Gather any templates for drawing you might have, they will help make your dividing lines nice and smooth. Cups and plates in different sizes work great, I like to use the same templates I use in my quilting.

Step 2: Reference Points

Find a nice flat surface. I like to use my drawing board that I picked up at the local craft supply store. Take your black and white print out and tape it to your flat surface using small amounts of painter's tape in each corner. Once your print out is secure you will want to make reference marks in each corner, I just use dots. You will then write top on the top of the page. Now, I take a look at the picture. I am specifically looking at the intersections of the piecing. I like to have "middle points" to work off of so if there is no piecing out towards the borders I will put a hash mark in the middle of the border. Tape a piece of tracing paper over your print out taking the time to make those same reference marks in case any of the layers shift, it is not necessary to make the "middle points" marks. The reference marks are extremely important, do not skip this step. It is rare that I draw what I like the first time around but I have found that I will sometimes go back to previous drawings. The reference marks make it very easy to line everything up again.

Step 3: Getting Started

Getting started is the hardest part. These dividing lines will be stitched out so you want them to be pleasing to the eye.

The center of the quilt is typically the focal point. I prefer to start all design work there. It is then easier to work those same shapes throughout the quilt in a more flowing and planned manner. You will use the piecing intersections as points to line up your templates. This way when you move to the quilt you will just use the same piecing intersections to line up your quilting template.

You'll notice that I am lining up the template from center of the negative square to center of the negative square. This way when I move to the quilt, I will do the same thing when I quilt it. I will likely have to use a different template as we have not been drawing to scale.

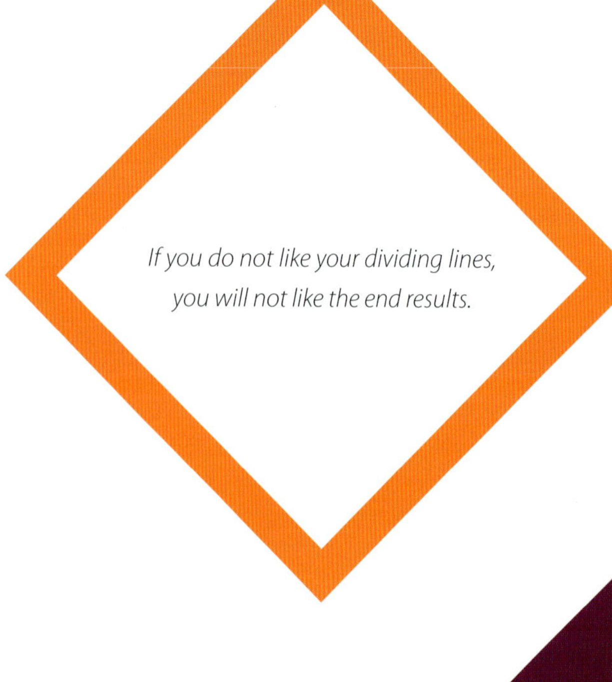

If you do not like your dividing lines, you will not like the end results.

I try not to over think this step. Just select a template and start drawing from one piecing intersection to another until you come up with some pleasing shape. You want to try and avoid making big sweeping lines with the templates as this will be hard to accomplish when you are quilting. Think small. I typically don't quilt over piecing lines, background piecing lines, yes but not the design piecing. This is not to say YOU can't quilt over the design piecing, just that I prefer not to. All of the lines you are drawing will be echo quilted ¼". So to get an idea of how it will look on the quilt, draw a line parallel to these lines. These parallel lines will create a wonderful design on the finished quilt. You love your dividing lines, time to grab an ultra-fine point Sharpie® and trace over these lines. You'll be happy you did as the more layers of tracing paper on top will make it difficult to see your lines. If my template will span the distance from the piecing intersections, I will not mark my quilt but if they don't I generally use a blue washout marker to mark it. I try to mark as little as possible so I don't have to worry about a bleeding quilt. If you are a domestic or hand quilter and you do not use templates while quilting, you may want to consider marking all of your dividing lines. The more dividing lines you have the more areas you will have to design for. This sometimes makes for a more intricate and interesting quilt. Just remember you haven't been drawing to scale so most likely you will need more than you think. This is why it helps to stitch out the dividing lines before continuing with the design process.

Step 4: Quilting

Once I have the dividing lines drawn, I will move to my machine and quilt them along with all of my stitch in the ditch work. You will need to be flexible because nothing has been drawn to scale. Choose a template to quilt with that will give you the closest look to what you have drawn. Stitching out all of the dividing lines will also make you aware of any areas that are too large. If you feel a section is larger than you'd like, go back to your paper and draw it out. You want the quilt to be completely stabilized when you finish quilting this part. If there are any areas larger than the size of a fist, take the time to pin baste. This will allow you to work on any area of the quilt you like in the next step. Quite often as I am quilting the dividing lines, ideas for quilting motifs will pop into my head. If this occurs, sketch it so you don't forget it!

Step 5: Open Space Design

Layer another sheet of tracing paper on top of the first and make those same reference marks. I know what you might be thinking. I'm going to save on some paper and just draw on the same sheet. While this is a good thought, learn from my mistakes. I typically draw a couple of designs out on a couple of different sheets of tracing paper, and then I chose the one I like the best. If you erase, you have to remember. Since I like to have areas within the quilt for the eye to rest I alternate placing design motifs with fill work. If you were to put design motifs in all of the areas, they will all be competing with each other for attention. By alternating the motifs with the fill work each of your motifs will have the opportunity to shine.

If you don't want it quilted to the hilt, think about making your quilting motifs larger so you won't have to do as much small time consuming background fill. If you are quilting on a customer quilt, keep their budget in mind. When choosing your design motifs, you can always look to the fabric for some inspiration. I love feathers so that is the motif I typically choose. However, there are numerous different feathers to choose from, formal to fun and flirty. I have had many students who don't know how to quilt any motifs, forego this step and move straight to the fill work and their quilts turned out fantastic.

Once I have them all drawn, I will then move back to my machine and quilt them. When choosing your thread for the designs, think about how much you want them to show or would you like them to be secondary to the piecing. A contrasting thread will have them show while a matching thread will have them become a secondary design.

Step 6: Deciding on Fills

Once the design motifs are quilted, layer another sheet of tracing paper and make the same reference marks. This is the last, but very important step - deciding what fills to use. As I mentioned earlier fills give the eye a place to rest. I like fill work to be repetitive and add texture to the quilt so an evenly spaced meander, small evenly spaced crosshatch or curved crosshatch, and my favorite, a straight line fill are all excellent options. I try and use a variety of fills as I find it lends interest to the quilt. The choices are limited only by your own imagination. I typically don't draw out the entire fill as it is as time consuming to draw as it is to quilt. I like to use a nice fine thread for fill work, especially the dense work as it won't look as "thready" and make your quilt feel like cardboard.

Be sure of your fill, removing this from your quilt is not fun and what takes 1 minute to put in, could take 1 hour to remove.

Over time Divide and Design will become your go-to method for planning the quilting on all your quilts. I hope that you find this design method useful in taking your custom quilting to the next level or to simply make the decisions about what to quilt easier. While I use this design method on my award winning quilts, I also use it on my day to day quilts to take something that might be a little simple and turn it into an eye catching heirloom.

Designing for Appliqué Quilts

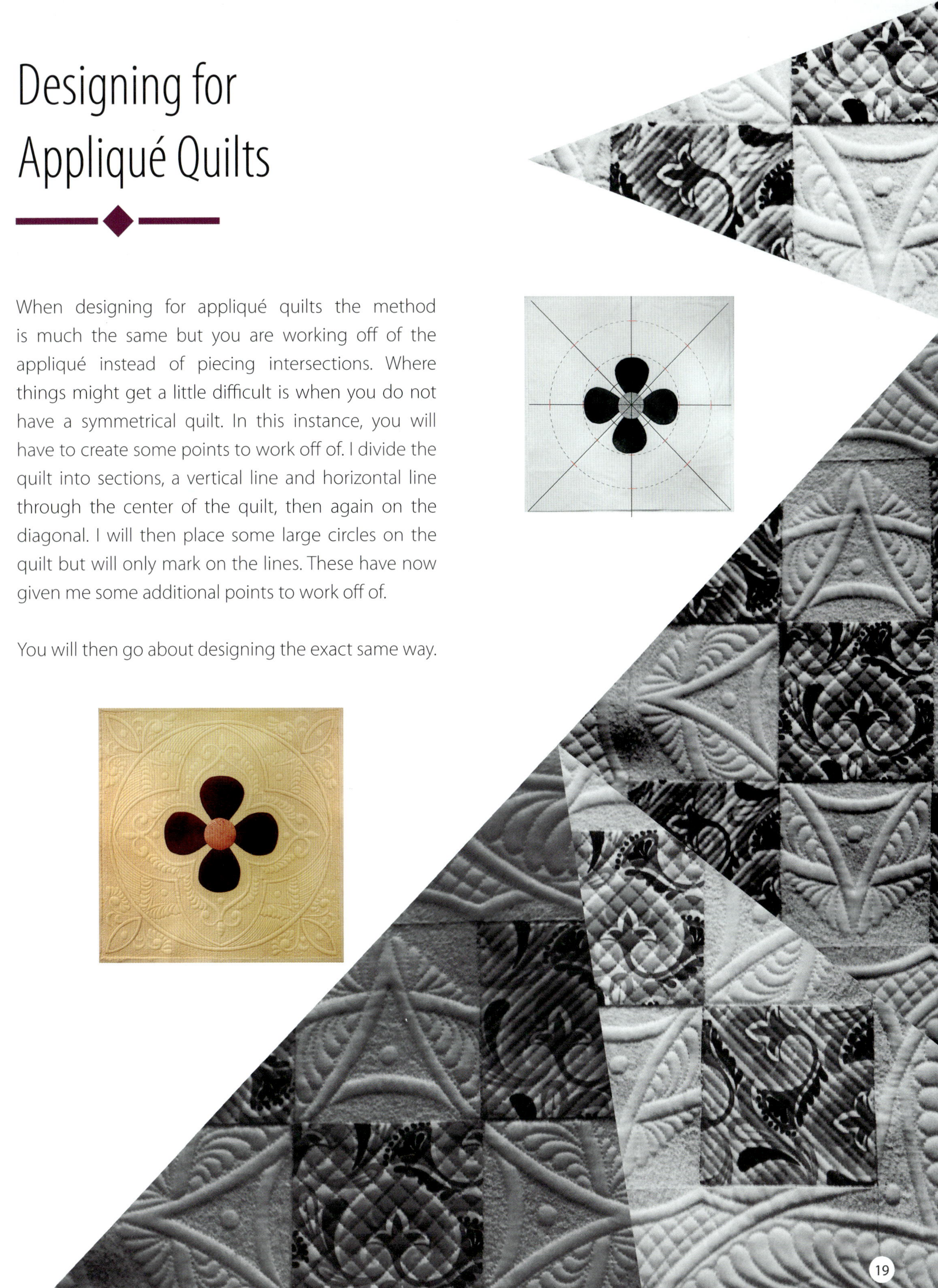

When designing for appliqué quilts the method is much the same but you are working off of the appliqué instead of piecing intersections. Where things might get a little difficult is when you do not have a symmetrical quilt. In this instance, you will have to create some points to work off of. I divide the quilt into sections, a vertical line and horizontal line through the center of the quilt, then again on the diagonal. I will then place some large circles on the quilt but will only mark on the lines. These have now given me some additional points to work off of.

You will then go about designing the exact same way.

Fabric, Batting, and Thread

Fabric Selection

When I choose fabrics for my projects, I often start with a busy large print as my inspiration and then look for coordinating fabrics. Nowadays the fabric lines are so great that I can often find what I am looking for in one line. The busy print normally becomes my border fabric and then I look for a smaller print for the piecing in the quilt. When it comes to the background fabric, I like to have a solid fabric so that the quilting will really show. If you choose something that has any elements to it, it will compete with the quilting which defeats the purpose of the extraordinary quilting that you are going to do. One thing is for sure use high quality fabrics for all of your projects. You want them to last more than a lifetime.

As for the color, that is completely up to you. You want to create a quilt that is striking? A nice dark color with a contrasting thread will surely turn heads. If you are looking for something a little more subtle then maybe go with a light color background with a thread to blend. There are so many different choices to make when creating a quilt. Consider taking those orphan blocks from various projects and quilt them up individually. This allows you to play with a small sample to see what you like and what you don't like. Give it a try. We all have those blocks just lying around.

Batting

When I first started quilting, I did not give a lot of thought to my batting. I figured it was just sandwiched between fabrics, what did it matter? It matters! Think about the end use of the quilt when choosing your batting. Is it a baby quilt? You might choose something that is flame retardant. Going to warm climate, try a nice light weight batting. These are some of the things you need to think about.

When quilting my competition pieces, I like to use two layers of batting as I am lazy and do not want to do Trapunto to give my quilt definition. I will use a base layer of polyester and a top layer of wool. The wool is what will give the quilting some dimension.

I do not normally use a really thin batting as it does not hold up well to the tugging that I do on my longarm. If you are a domestic or a hand quilter, this might be the perfect choice.

If the batting isn't something that I would want to curl up with on its own, it probably isn't something that I am going to use in my quilt.

Thread

When I was quilting for customers, I pretty much found the thread that worked in my machine with no fussing and I stuck with it for 10 years. Now I am starting to play around with different threads and having a ball. There are so many on the market to choose from but just like you want high quality fabric, the same is for the thread. You will have fewer headaches with a high quality thread.

Your first decision when choosing a thread is the obvious, color. Are you looking to make a splash or just a mild wave? A contrasting thread will scream come look at me, while a thread that blends will add a nice complement to the quilt. When I choose a thread to blend, I want to try and go either a shade darker or lighter than the background.

Once you have the color, you might have to decide on the weight of thread. They range from 12-wt being a very thick thread to 100-wt being a super fine thread. Each will have a place in your quilt. A thicker thread looks great as your dividing lines while 100-wt is perfect for a dense background fill.

How about those specialty threads? The metallic threads also look great as the dividing lines or for doing some fun bobbin work. They are those threads that are too heavy to go through the needle and you wind them on your bobbin and quilt from the back.

Keep the end use of the quilt in mind when choosing your thread. You would not want to use a metallic or do bobbin work on a quilt that is meant for a baby or to be cuddled with. Save those threads for the wall hangings.

Choosing the Right Template

You have not been drawing to scale so you will not use the same size templates that you used in the drawing. When you do go to select your template, you will want to make sure that you are selecting one that gives you the same look as what you have drawn. Remember that if you are using the ruler to quilt with (not just mark), the hopping foot adds ¼".

Two of the most common errors I come across in my classes when selecting the appropriate template is choosing an arc that is too small to create a line, thus creating an area where the two lines overlap or choosing one that isn't deep enough and it comes across as a straight line. You will want to be aware of this as you pick your templates.

Templates are very common in the longarm world and are just starting to gain traction in domestic machine quilting. The precision you get when using templates is wonderful, especially for those of us that are challenged with following a predrawn line. If you are a domestic quilter, give it a try. Grab one of those orphan blocks you have lying around and play around. You will want to make sure that you put something on the bottom of your templates so that they move along with the fabric.

The Projects

Pg. 30

Pg. 48

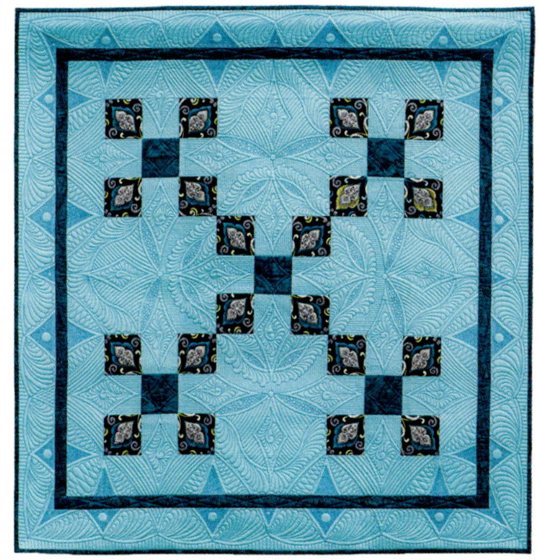
Pg. 72

Pg. 60

Pg. 86

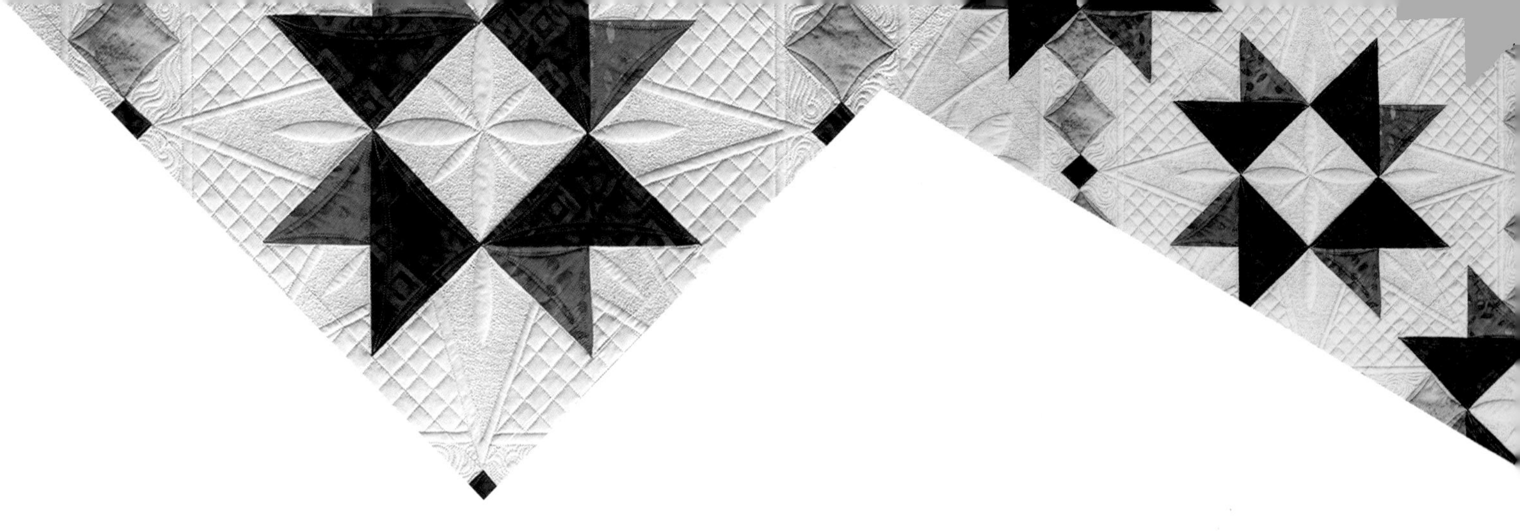

Lavish

46" x 46"

12" Blocks

Fabric

- Light Purple: ⅓ yard
- Orange: ⅜ yard
- Dark Purple: ½ yard
- White: 2¼ yd

Cutting Instructions

Light Purple-

- Cut (2) strips 2½" x WOF
  Subcut into (32) 2½" squares
- Cut (2) strips 3" x WOF
  Subcut into (24) 3" x 3" squares

Orange-

- Cut (1) strip 5½" x WOF
  Subcut into (5) 5¼" squares
  Subcut from Corner to Corner for (20) triangles
- Cut (2) strips 1¾" x WOF
  Subcut into (24) 1¾" squares

Dark Purple-

- Cut (2) strips 4⅞" x WOF
  Subcut into (10) 4⅞" squares
  Subcut on the Diagonal for (20) triangles
- Cut (4) strips 34½" x 6½"

Sashing -

- Cut (1) strip 1½" x WOF
  Subcut into (12) 1½" squares
- Cut (2) strips 1¾" x WOF
  Subcut into (24) 1¾" squares

Cutting Instructions (Continued)

White Fabric -

- Cut (2) strips 2½" x WOF
  - Subcut (32) 2½" squares
- Cut (1) strip 5¼" x WOF
  - Subcut (5) 5¼" squares
  - Subcut from Corner to Corner for (20) triangles
- Cut (2) strips 4½" x WOF
  - Subcut into (9) 4½" squares
- Sashing: Cut (6) strips 1½" x WOF
  - Subcut into (16) 1½" x 12½" rectangles
- Setting Triangles: Cut (1) 19¾" square
  - Subcut from Corner to Corner for (4) triangles
- Cut (2) 10⅞" squares
  - Subcut from corner to corner for (4) triangles
- Cut (2) strips 1" x 38½"
- Cut (2) strips 1" x 40"
- Cut (7) strips 2⅝" x WOF
  - Subcut into (96) 2⅝" x 2⅝" squares,
  - Subcut once on diagonal for (192) triangles
- Cut (3) strips 1¾" x WOF

Piecing Instructions

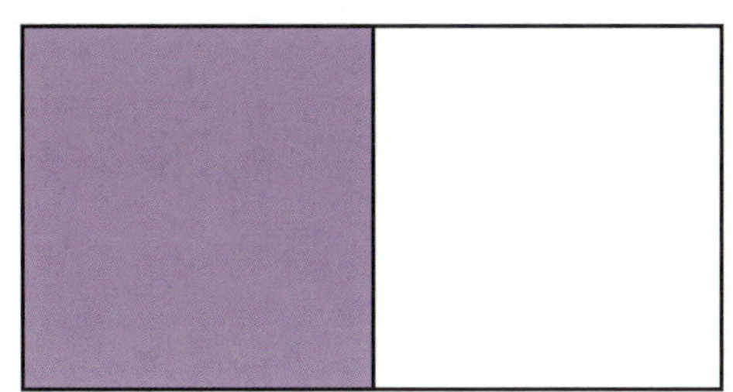

1. Sew (32) Light Purple 2½" squares to (32) White 2½" squares. Press.

2. Sew these units together to create (16) 4 patch units. Press.

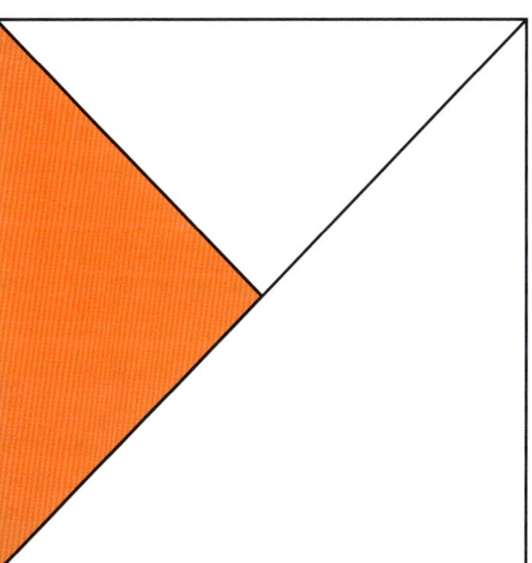

3. Sew (20) Orange triangles to (20) White triangles. Press.

4. Sew the Orange/White unit to (20) Dark Purple triangles. Press.

5. Sew (7) Dark Purple/Orange units to (5) white 4½" squares. Press.

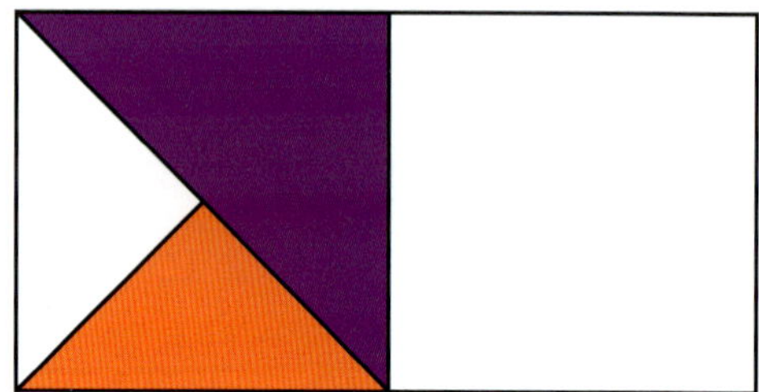

6. Sew (5) Dark Purple/Orange units to the above unit. Press.

7. For center star: Sew (1) White 4½" square to the unit from step 5. Make (2) units. Press.

8. Sew these (2) units to either side of the unit from step 6. Press. You will only have one block.

9. Sew (8) 4 patch blocks to the unit from step 4. Press. (Watch placement of the 4 patch).

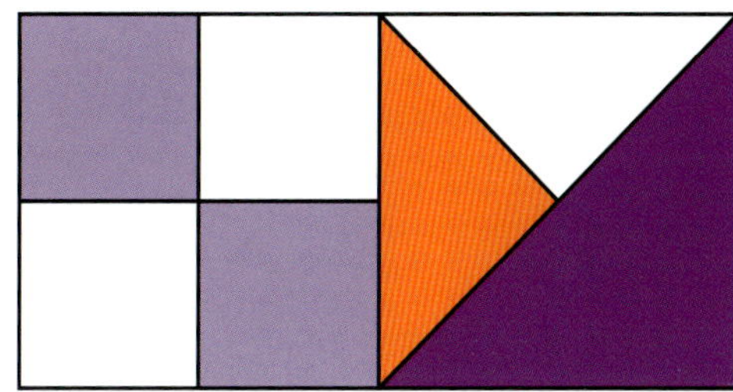

10. Sew another 4 patch to the unit from step 9. Press. (Again watch placement of 4 patch) You will have 8 units.

11. Sew the unit from step 9 to unit from step 6. Make (4) units. Press.

12. Sew the remainder of the units from step 9 to the unit from step 10. Make (4) units and press.

13. Sew (6) Dark Purple 1½" squares to (6) 1½" x 12½" White rectangles. Press

14. Sew (6) Dark Purple 1½" squares to other end of above unit. Press.

15. Sew (2) 1½" x 12½" White rectangles to both sides of unit from step 8. Press.

16. Sew (2) units from step 13 to both sides of the unit from step 14. Press.

17. Sew (2) White 1½" x 12½" squares to both sides of the unit from step 11. Press.

18. Sew (1) sashing unit from step 13 to one side of unit from step 16. Make (4) units. Press.

19. Sew (2) units from step 13 to both sides of the unit from step 14. Press.

20. Sew (2) White 1½" x 12½" squares to both sides of the unit from step 11. Press.

21. Sew (2) small White setting triangles to the unit from step 19. Make 2 units. Press.

22. Sew remaining (2) small White setting triangles to both ends of unit from step 18. Press.

23. Sew (2) units from step 20 to either side of unit from step 21. Press.

24. Sew 1" x 38½" White border to two sides of quilt top. Press.

25. Sew 1" x 40" White border to remaining two sides. Press.

26. Sew (24) White 1¾" squares to (24) Orange 1¾" squares. Press

27. Sew (24) White 1¾" squares to (24) Dark Purple 1¾" squares. Press

28. Sew unit from step 25 and 26 together to create (48) 4 patches. Press.

29. Sew a White triangle to each side of the 4 patches. Press.

30. Sew a White triangle to each side of the Light Purple 3" square. Press.

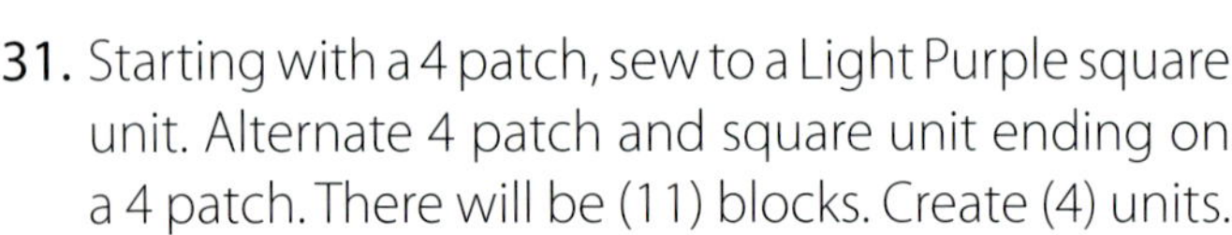

31. Starting with a 4 patch, sew to a Light Purple square unit. Alternate 4 patch and square unit ending on a 4 patch. There will be (11) blocks. Create (4) units.

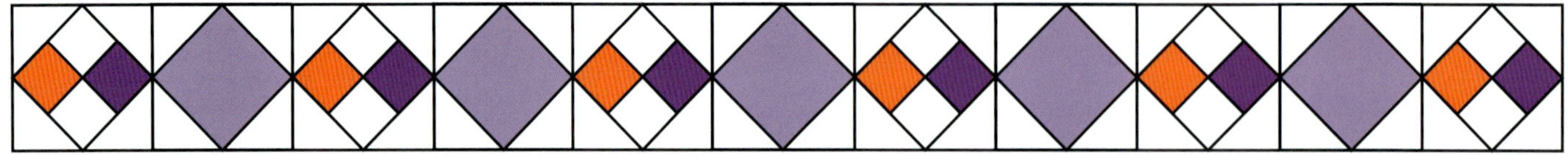

32. Sew (2) of the remaining (4) square units to (2) ends of one of the above units. Create 2.

33. Sew border units onto quilt top.

Assembly Diagram

Summer Solstice

46" x 46"
12" Blocks

Fabric

- Floral: ¼ yard
- Orange: ½ yard
- Stripe/Binding: ¾ yard
- Background: 1 yd

Cutting Instructions

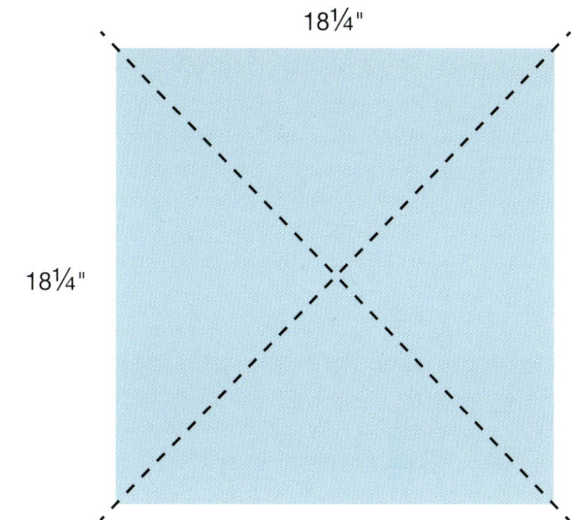

Floral-

- Cut (1) strip 4½" x WOF
  Subcut into (5) 4½" squares

Orange-

- Cut (2) strips 5" x WOF
  Subcut into (10) 5" squares
- Cut (1) strip 6½" x WOF
  Subcut into (4) ½" squares

Stripe-

- Cut (1) strip 2½" x WOF
  Subcut into (16) 2½" squares
- Cut (4) strips 34½" x 6½"

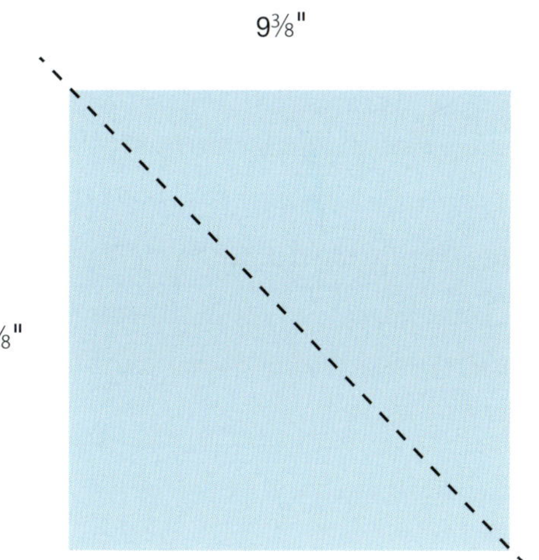

Background-

- Cut (2) strips 5" x WOF
  Subcut into (10) 5" squares and (4) 4½" squares
- Cut 1 strip 2½" x WOF
  Subcut into (16) 2½" squares
- Cut (1) strip 4½" x WOF
  Subcut into (16) 2½" x 4½"
- Cut (1) stip 18¼" x WOF
  Subcut into (1) 18¼" square and (2) 9⅜" squares

  Subcut 18¼" square diagonally from corner to corner,

  then the other corner to corner to create (4) setting triangles

  Subcut the (2) 9⅜" squares diagonally from one corner
  to corner creating (2) corner triangles from each square.

Sewing Instructions

1. Take the 5" Background squares and draw a line from corner to corner. Repeat on (10) squares.

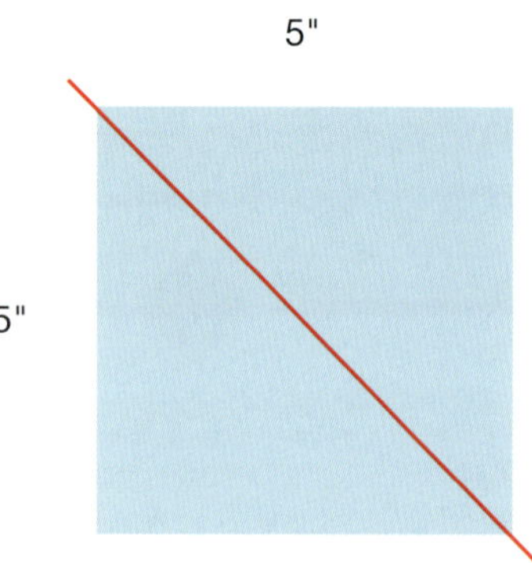

2. Layer these (10) squares right sides together with the Orange fabric. Sew ¼" away from drawn lines on both sides. Cut each of the (10) units on the drawn line. Press towards the Orange fabric. This should yield you (20) ½" square triangles.

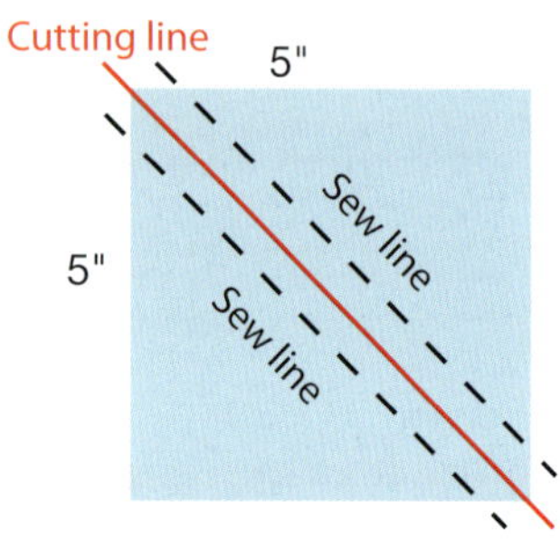

3. Sew Striped 2½" square to Background 2½" square. Repeat with remaining (15). Press towards the Stripe fabric. Sew that unit to the Background 2½" x 4½". Repeat with remaining (15) units. This should measure 4½" x 4½".

4. Sew (2) half square triangles to both sides of 4½" square of Floral fabric. Repeat for remaining (4).

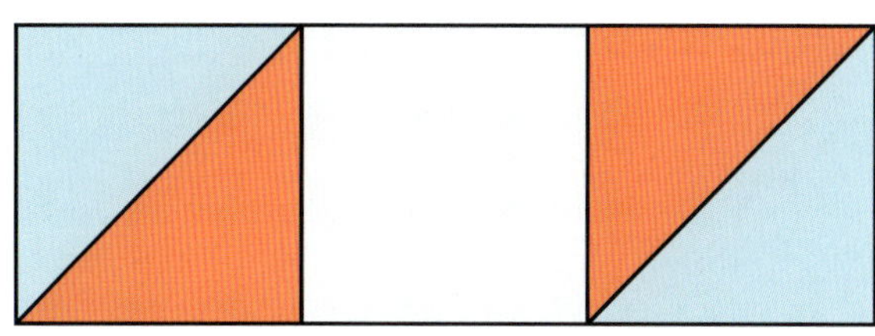

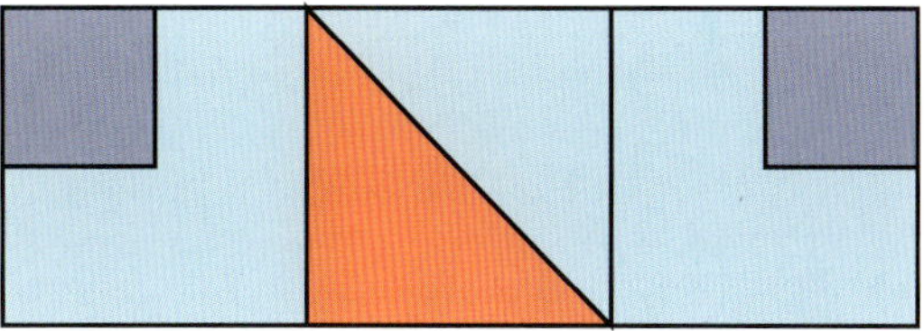

5. Sew the block you created in step 3 to both sides of half square triangles. Stripe fabric should be in outer corner. Press toward half square triangles. Make (8) units.

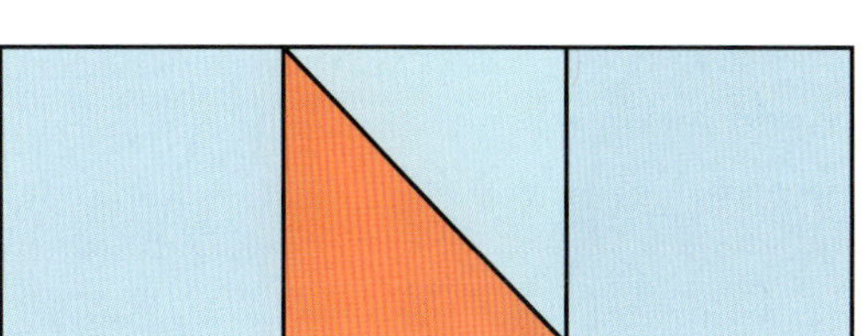

6. Sew (2) 4½" Background squares to both sides of (2) half square triangles. Sew these (2) units to Floral fabric unit to create your center friendship star. Make (2).

7. Sew the Stripe fabric units to the remaining (4) Floral fabric units to create (4) outer stars.

8. Sew (1) setting triangle to both sides of friendship star. Repeat with (1) more friendship star.

9. Sew smaller corner triangle to this unit. Repeat.

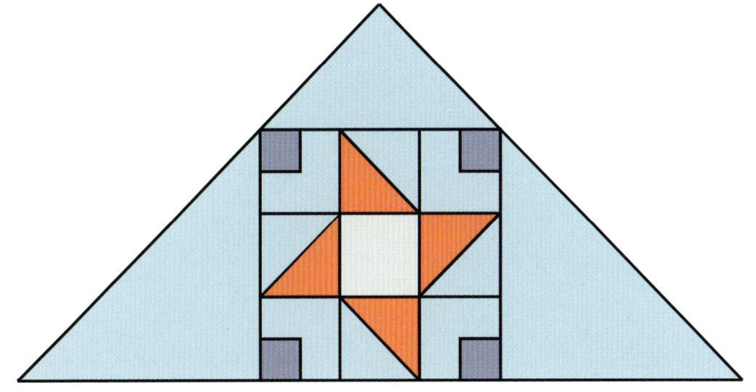

10. Sew (1) friendship star block to both sides of center friendship star block. Sew (1) corner triangle to each end.

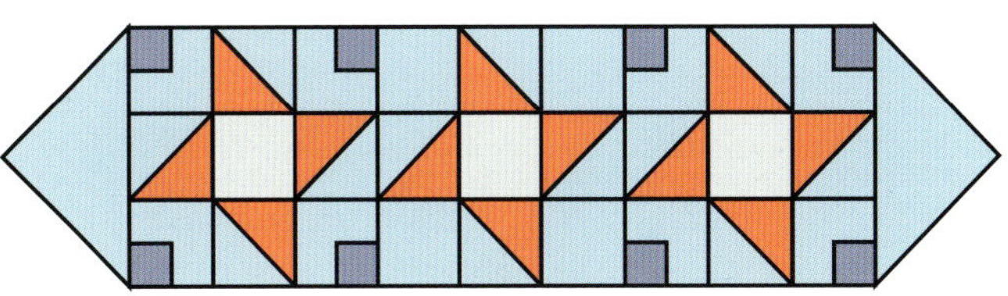

11. Sew (3) units together, carefully matching seams.

12. Sew an Orange 6½" x 6½" square to each side of Stripe 6½" x 34½".

13. Sew a Stripe 6½" x 34½" piece to each side of the interior unit. Then sew the unit created above to each side.

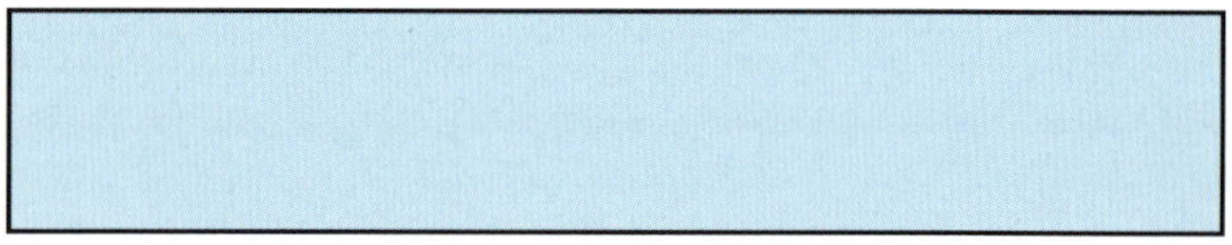

Assembly Diagram

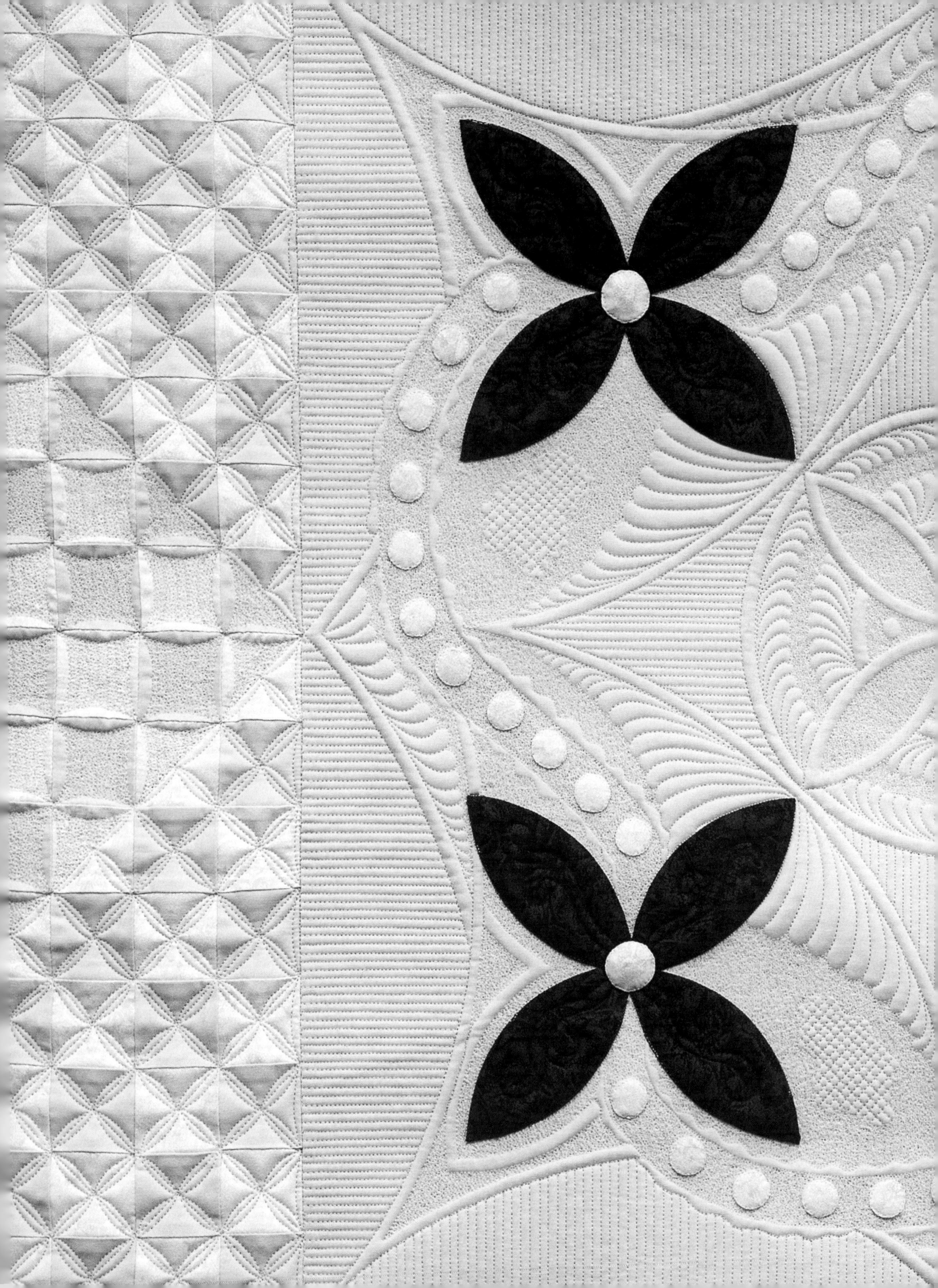

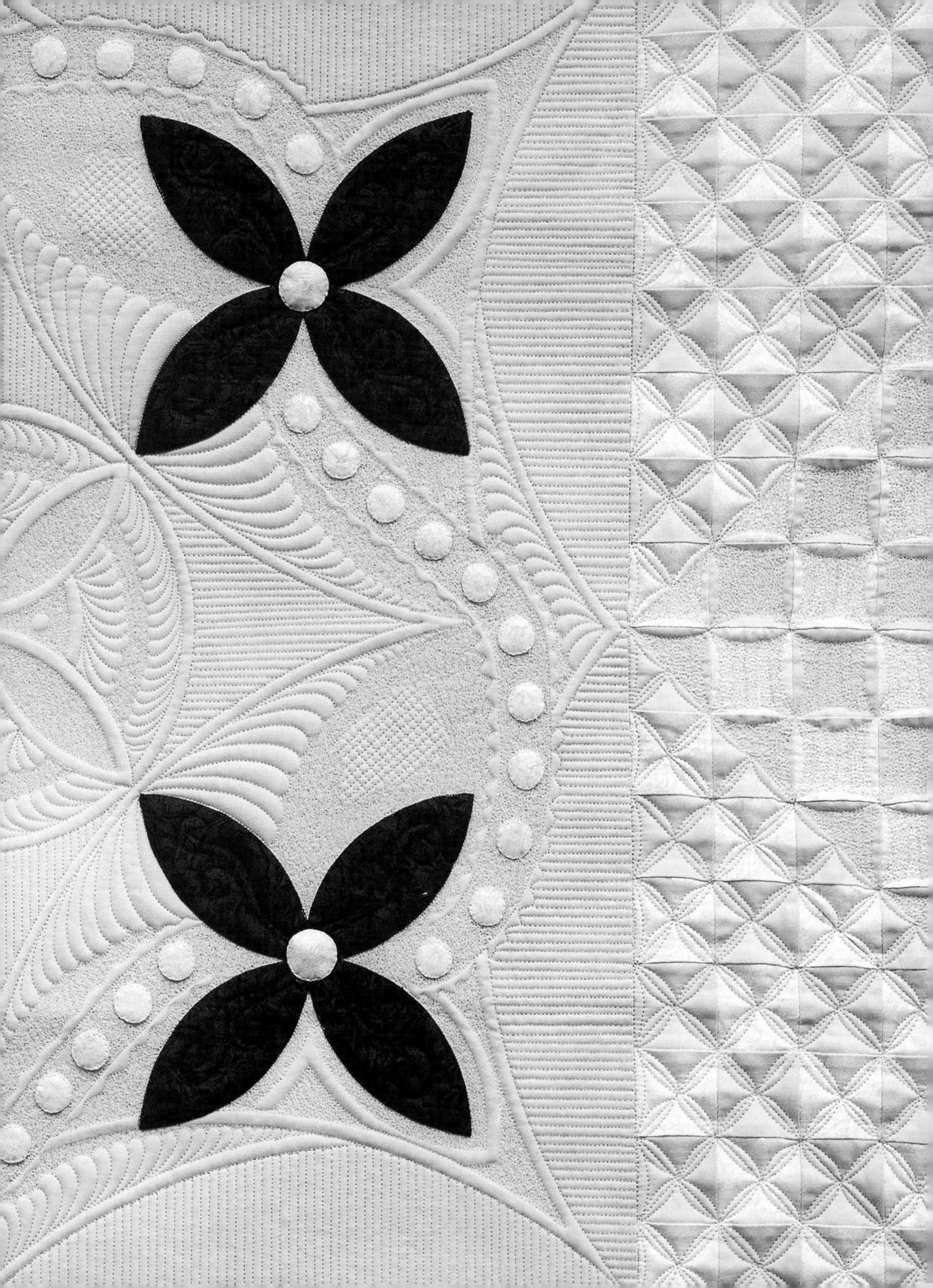

Petit a Four

36" x 36"

Fabric

- Solid Pink: 1¼ yard
- Pink Print: ¾ yard
- Black: ½ yard
- Binding Fabric: ¼ yard
- Backing: 1¼ yard

Tools

- Marvy® Uchida Fabric Marker
- Elmer's® Washable School Glue
- 1 sheet of Templar®
- Karen Kay Buckley's Perfect Circles®
- Magic® Sizing or Starch
- Stencil Brush
- Iron
- Monofilament thread

Cutting Instructions

Solid Pink-
- Cut (1) 24½" square
- Cut (8) 2" x WOF strips

Pink Print-
- Cut (8) 2" x WOF strips
- Cut (1) 2" x WOF strip,
  Subcut into (16) 2" x 3½" rectangles
- Cut (4) large circles
- Cut (44) medium circle

Black-
- Cut (4) 6½" squares
- Cut (2) 3" x WOF strip
  Subcut into (16) 3" x 6" rectangles
- Cut (4) small circles adding ⅜" seam allowance

Strip Sets

Make 8

Make 4

1. Sew (1) 2" Solid Pink strip and (1) 2" Printed Pink strip lengthwise. Make (8) strip sets. Press the seams towards the Solid Pink. Sew strip sets together as shown to the left.

Make 64

2. Cut strip sets horizontally to create (64) units measuring 2" x 6½".

3. Sew 2" x 6½" units together to create (32) units measuring 3½" x 6½". Press to one side. Then sew 3½" x 6½" units together to create (16) units measuring 6½" square unit as show on the right. Press.

Make 32

Make 16

4. Sew (4) 6½" square units together to create (4) units.

Make 4

Appliqué Pieces

Use a ⅜" seam allowance on all appliqué shapes.

Pink Print-

- Template #1- 16 pieces
- Template #2 - 44 pieces
- Template #3 - 4 pieces

Black-

- Template #4 - 16 pieces
- Template #5 - 4 pieces

Instructions:

1. Prepare appliqué pieces as described in the appliqué section of the book.

2. Once your appliqué pieces are prepared.

3. Using the layout guide place your pieces from Template 2, 3, and 4 onto your large piece of Solid Pink. Once you have them set, glue them in place using a small amount of Elmer's glue.

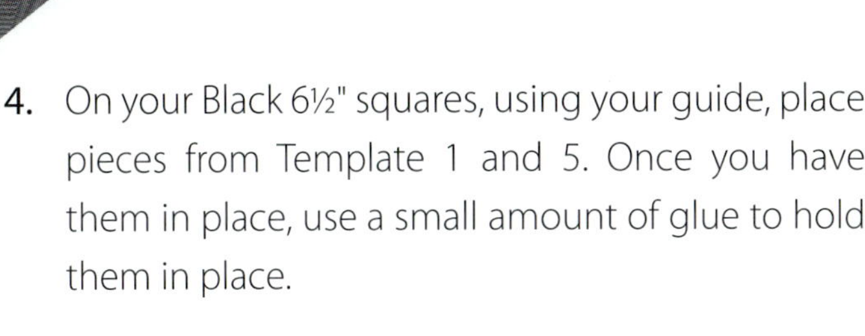

4. On your Black 6½" squares, using your guide, place pieces from Template 1 and 5. Once you have them in place, use a small amount of glue to hold them in place.

5. You are now ready to sew them onto your fabric. Refer to the appliqué section on what settings I used on my machine.

6. Sew (2) of your 16 patch block units to the large appliqué unit.

7. Sew (2) of your Black blocks to the two ends of your 16 patch unit. Make (2).

8. Sew these (2) units to the larger unit.

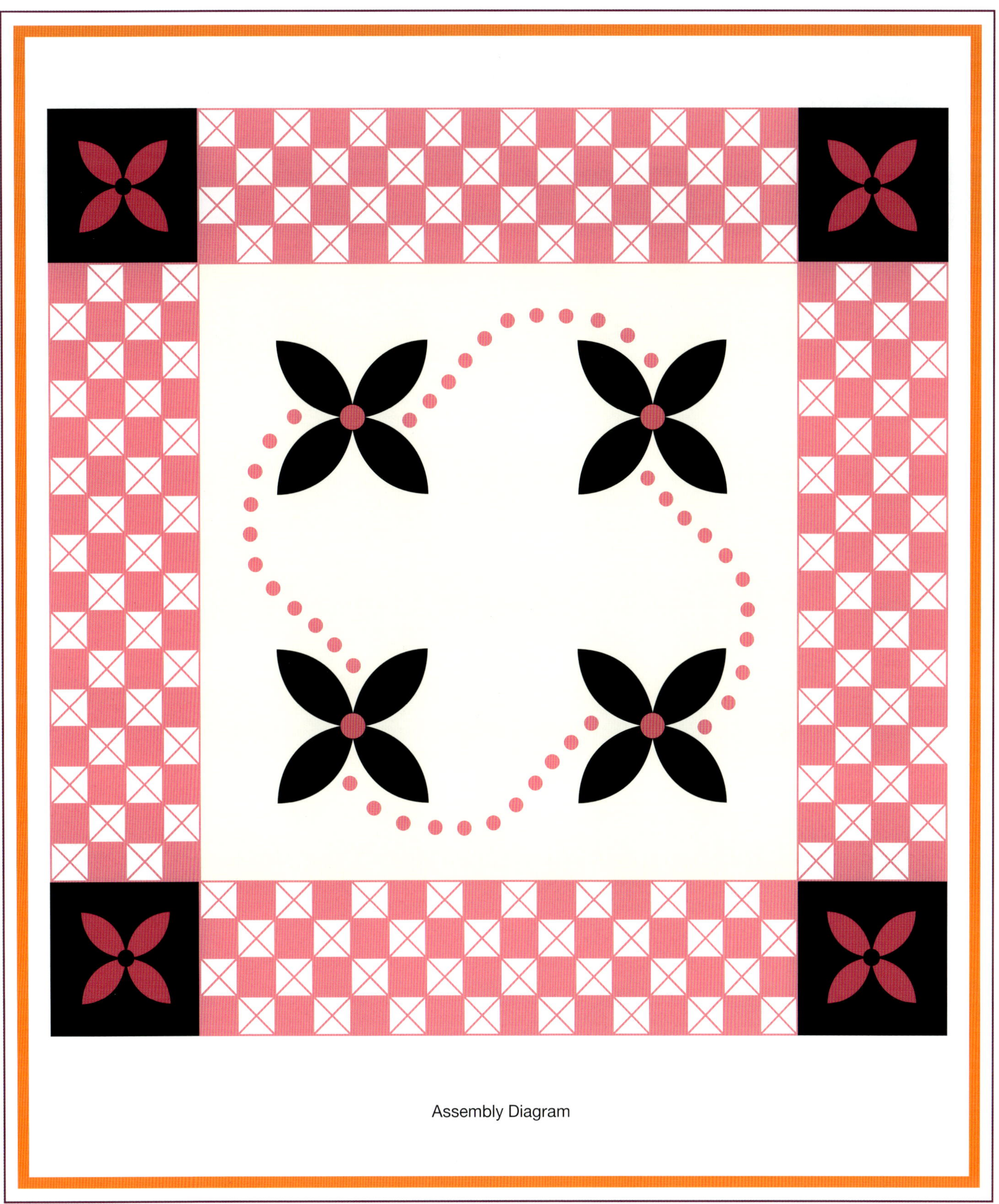

Assembly Diagram

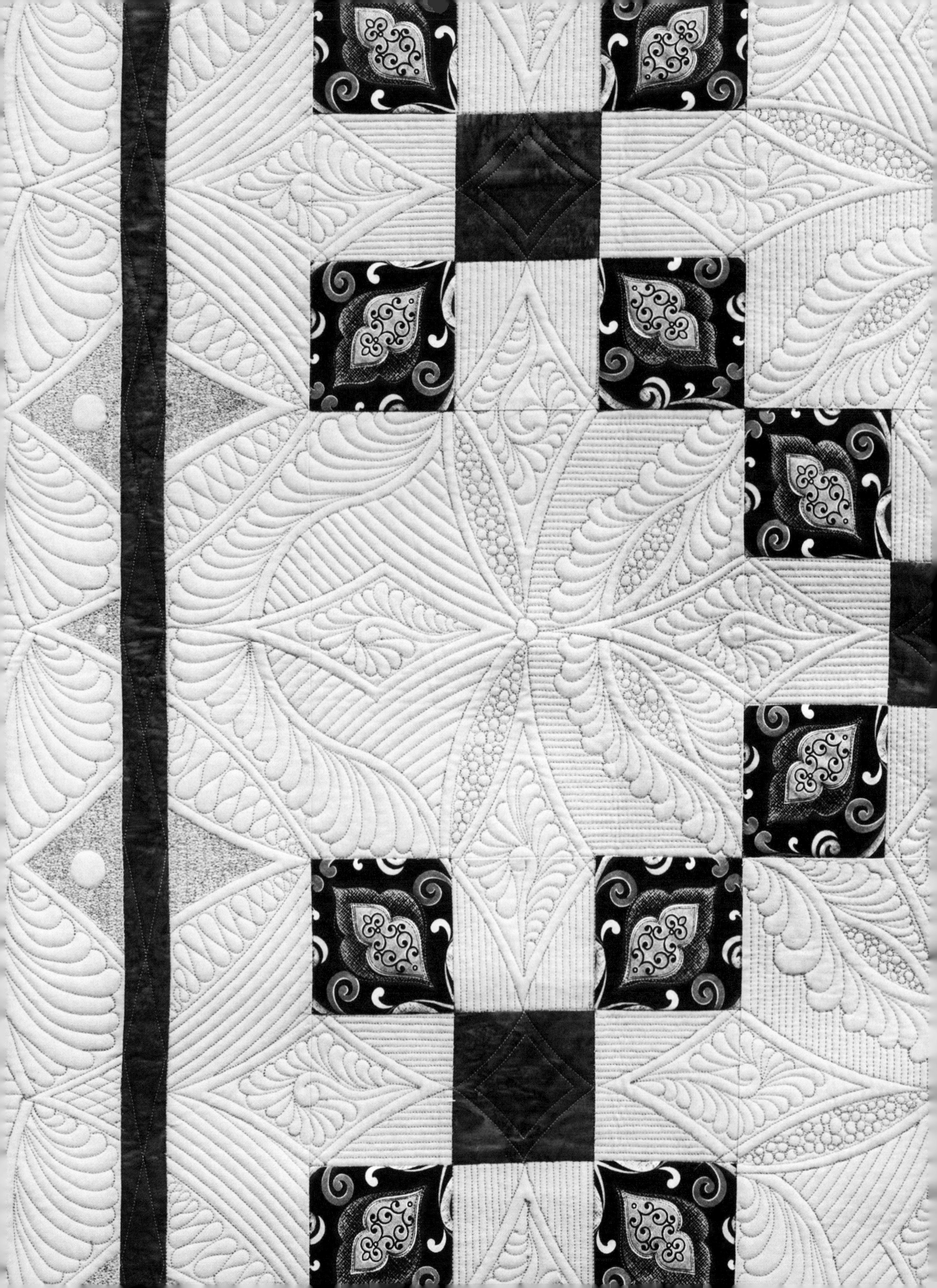

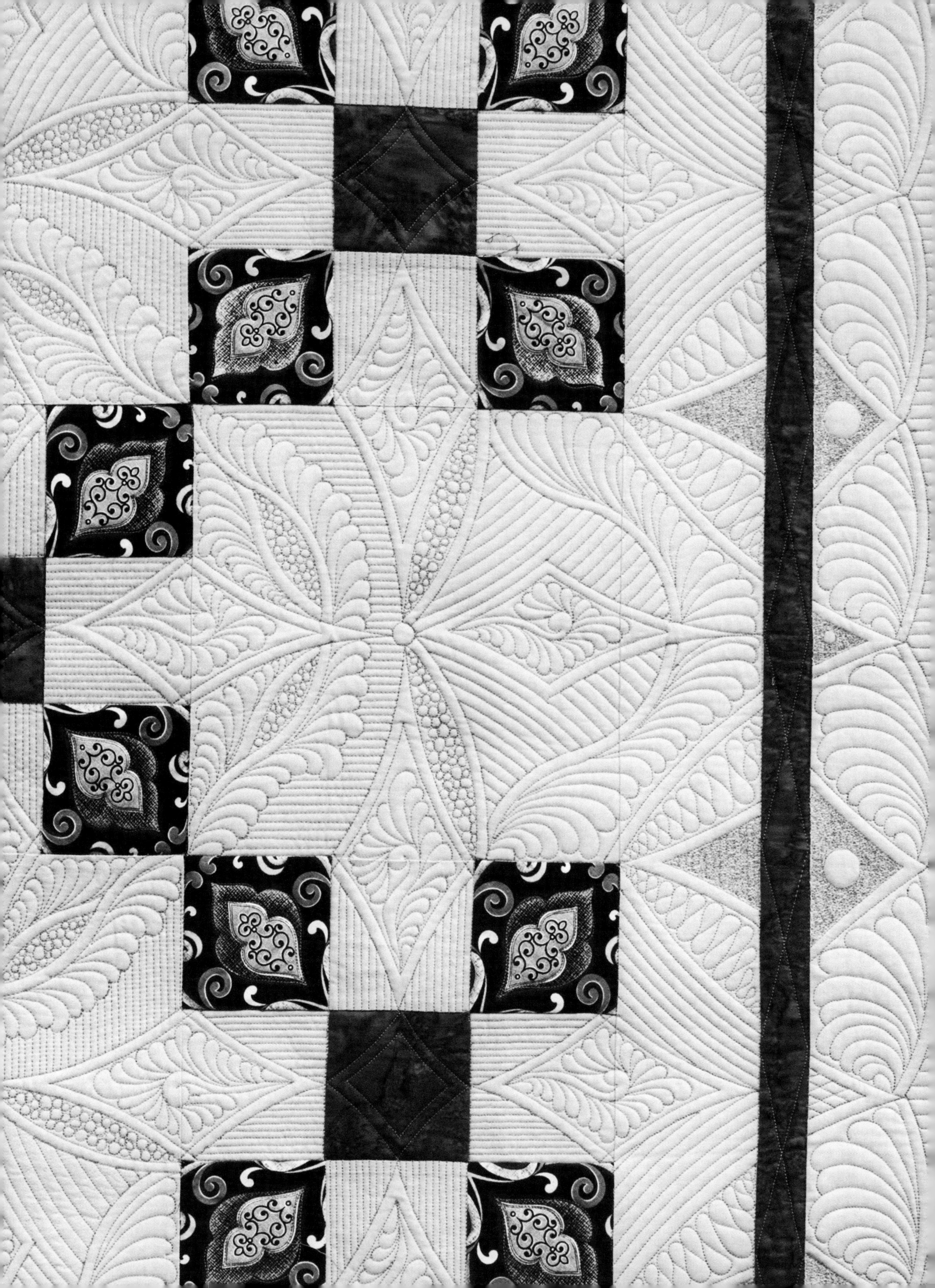

Checkmate

Turquoise Quilt : Finished 41" x 41"

Fabric

- Turquoise: 1½ yards
- Dark Turquoise: ¾ yard (includes binding)
- Print Fabric: ¼ yard
- Backing: 1¼ yard

Cutting Instructions

Turquoise-

- Cut (4) 9½" squares
- Cut (20) 3½" squares
- Cut (2) 3½" x 27½" strips
- Cut (2) 3½" x 33½" strips
- Cut (2) 3½" x 35½" strips
- Cut (2) 3½" x 41½" strips

Dark Turquoise-

- Cut (5) 3½" squares
- Cut (2) 1½" x 22½" strips
- Cut (2) 1½" x 24½" strips

Binding-

- Cut (5) 2½" x WOF strips

Print Fabric-

- Cut (20) 3½" squares

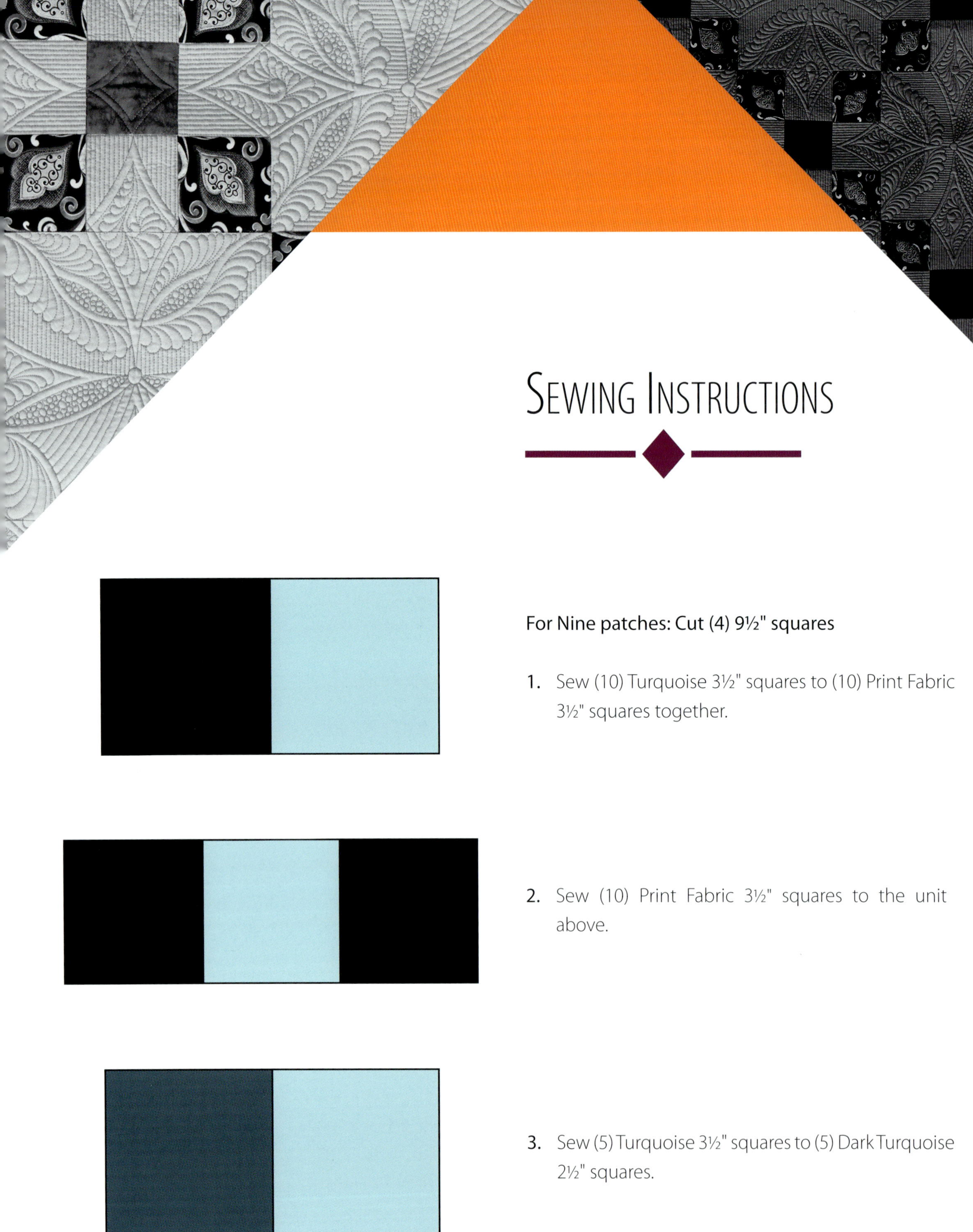

SEWING INSTRUCTIONS

For Nine patches: Cut (4) 9½" squares

1. Sew (10) Turquoise 3½" squares to (10) Print Fabric 3½" squares together.

2. Sew (10) Print Fabric 3½" squares to the unit above.

3. Sew (5) Turquoise 3½" squares to (5) Dark Turquoise 2½" squares.

4. Sew (5) Turquoise 3½" squares to the above unit.

5. Sew (1) unit from step 5 to (1) unit from step 7. Make (5) units.

6. Sew remaining step 5 units to step 8 units. Make (5) units.

7. Sew (1) Turquoise 9½" square to the unit from step 9. Make (3) units.

8. Sew remaining Turquoise 9½" square to opposite side of nine patch in above unit.

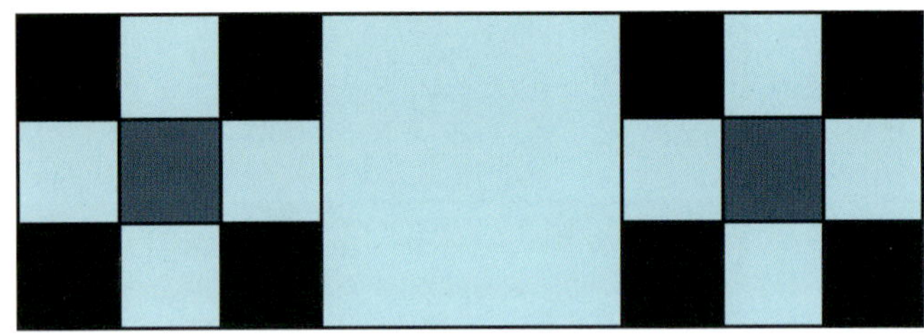

9. Sew nine patch unit to the unit from step 10. Make (2) units.

10. Sew nine patch unit to the unit from step 10. Make (2) units.

11. Sew (1) unit from step 12 to unit from step 11.

12. Sew remaining unit from step 12 to bottom of unit from step 13.

13. Sew (2) Turquoise 3½" x 27½" strips to above unit.

14. Sew (2) Turquoise 3½" x 33½" strip to above unit.

15. Sew (2) Dark Turquoise 1½" x 33½" strip to above unit.

16. Sew (2) Dark Turquoise 1½" x 35½" strip to above unit.

17. Sew (2) Turquoise 3½" x 33½" strip to above unit.

18. Sew (2) Turquoise 3½" x 35½" strip to above unit. Then sew remaining (2) Turquoise 3½" x 41½" strips on.

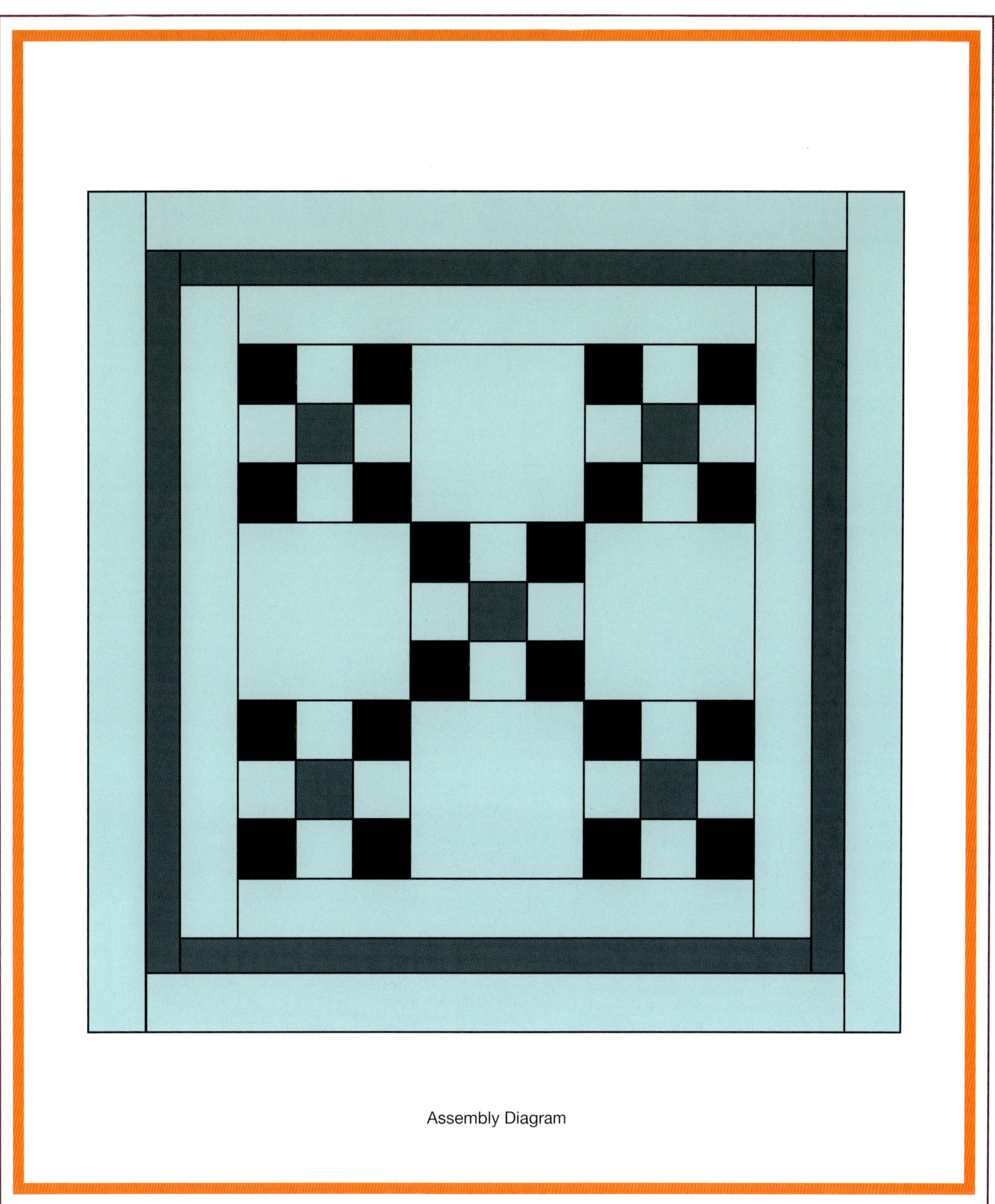

Assembly Diagram

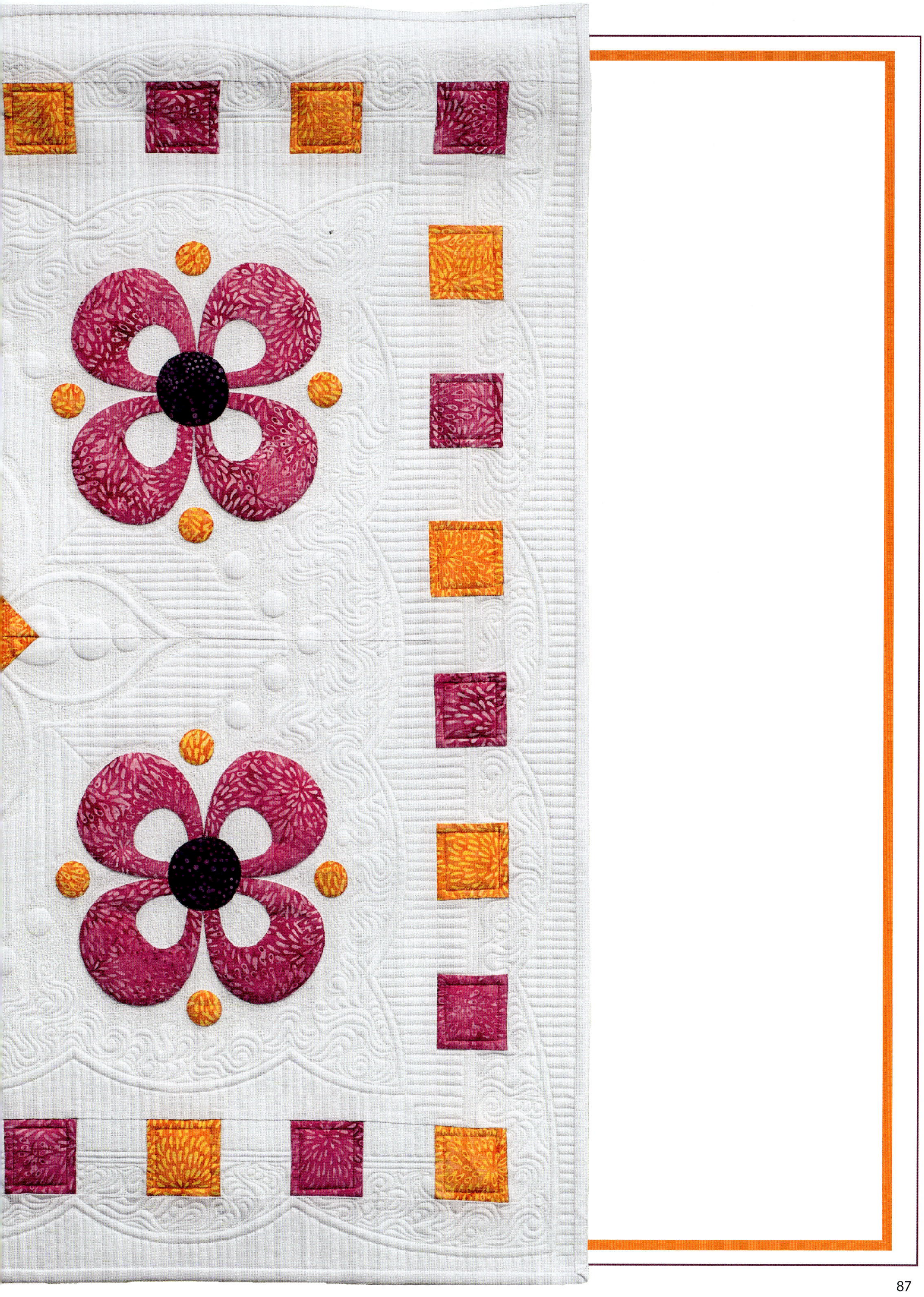

Lucky Blooms

32½" x 32½"

Fabric

- White Background: 1¼ yards
- Orange: ⅛ yard
- Pink: ⅓ yard
- Purple: Fat Quarter

Cutting Instructions

White Background-

- Cut (4) 13½" squares
- Cut (2) 2½" x WOF
  Subcut (28) 2½" squares
- Cut (2) 2½" x 30½"
- Cut (2) 2½" x 34½"

Orange Fabric-

- Cut (1) 2½" x WOF
  Subcut (20) 2½" squares
- Cut (16) 1½" circles

Pink Fabric-

- Cut (1) 2½" x WOF
  Subcut (14) 2½" squares
- Cut (2) 4½" x WOF
  Subcut (16) 4½" squares

Purple Fabric-

- Cut (1) 2½" x WOF
  Subcut (4) 2½" squares

Sewing Instructions

1. Prepare appliqué pieces using the method described in this book or your favorite.

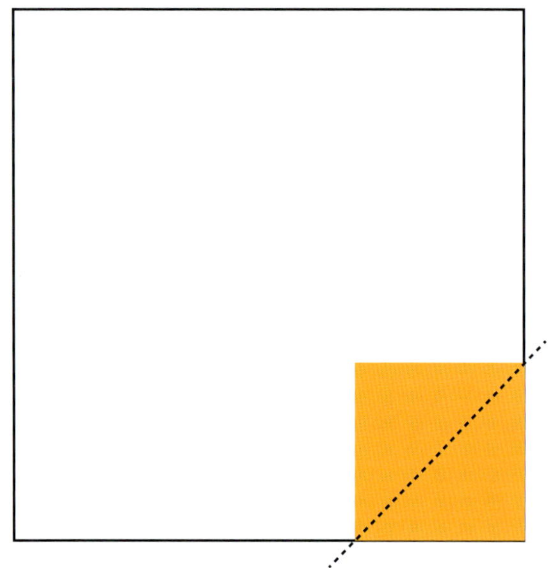

2. Mark the center of 13½" White Background squares, layer (1) 2½" Orange square in the corner of the 13½" square and sew on the diagonal. Trim and press. Repeat (3) more times for a total of (4) units.

3. Following guide adhere appliqué pieces to the above units.

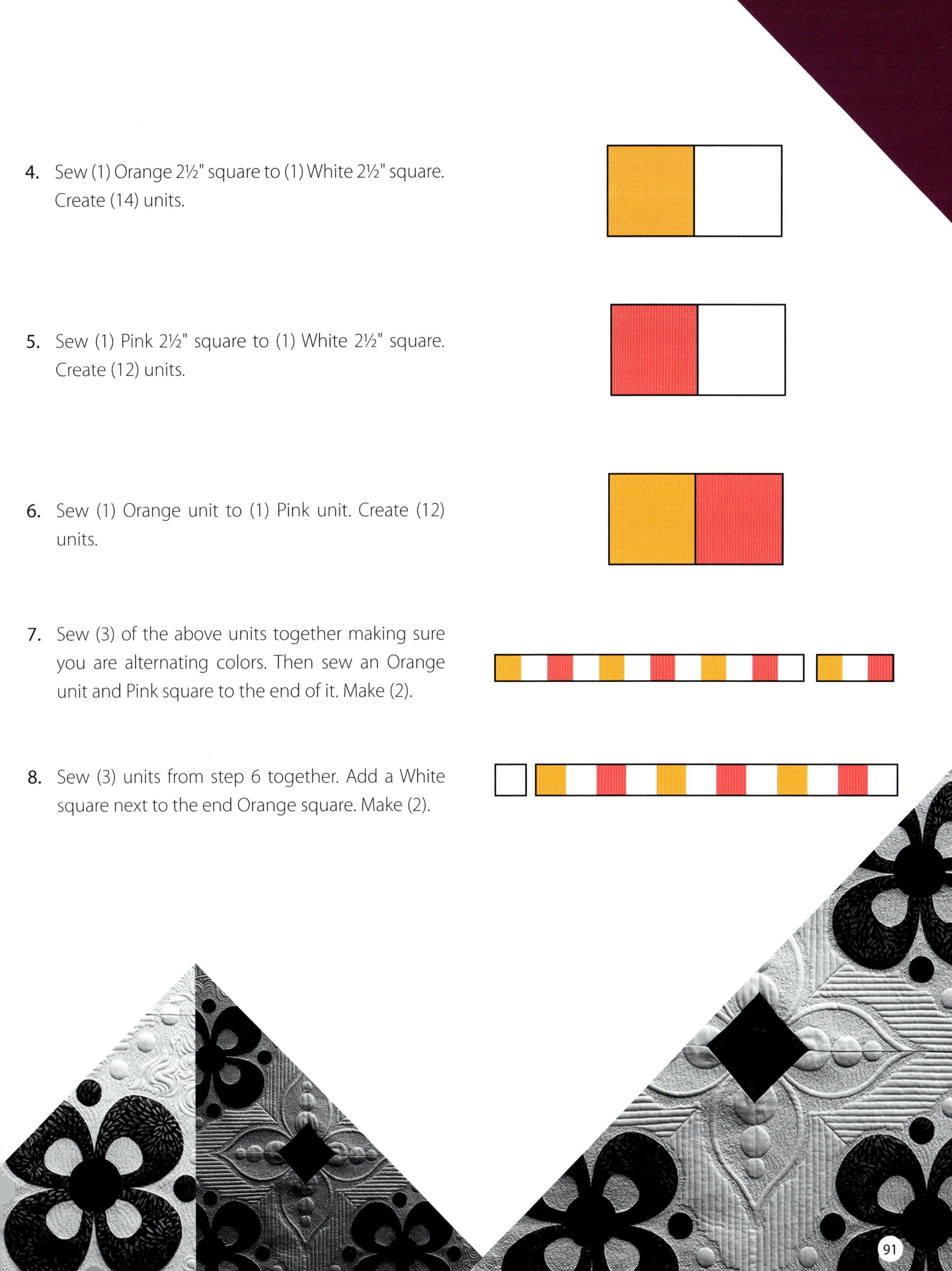

4. Sew (1) Orange 2½" square to (1) White 2½" square. Create (14) units.

5. Sew (1) Pink 2½" square to (1) White 2½" square. Create (12) units.

6. Sew (1) Orange unit to (1) Pink unit. Create (12) units.

7. Sew (3) of the above units together making sure you are alternating colors. Then sew an Orange unit and Pink square to the end of it. Make (2).

8. Sew (3) units from step 6 together. Add a White square next to the end Orange square. Make (2).

9. Sew the (4) blocks of appliqué together creating a square in the center with the Orange fabric.

10. Sew (2) border units on.

11. Sew on (2) other pieced border units.

12. Sew on remaining White borders.

13. Quilt using the divide and design method.

Assembly Diagram

About the author

Lisa H. Calle is a 1991 graduate of Philadelphia College of Textiles and Science with a BS in Textile Management and Marketing. She found a love for quilting in 1997 after leaving a management career in retail with the Limited Corporation's Bath & Body Works Division in 1999 to focus on raising a family.

Lisa resides in beautiful Chester County, Pennsylvania with her husband and three children. Her love for quilting is only surpassed by love of family and maybe golf.

Longarm Quilting Business

In 2004, Lisa first learned about longarm quilting machines while working part-time in the local quilt shop. Within weeks Stone House Quilting was accepting customers. Lisa finished quilts for 100's of clients, most of which are repeat customers. She has finished the annual Christmas quilt for several years for the prestigious Longwood Gardens in Kennett Square, Pa.

Designer

In 2005, Lisa's first paper pantographs were being sold through Willow Leaf studio, one of the first online pantograph stores. Since that time her portfolio of both paper and digital blocks, borders, fills, and sets have grown to 100's of choices available through a variety of online outlets including her own website, Urban Elementz, Digitechpatterns, Quilts Complete, and others.

Award Winning Quilter

In 2006, Lisa won her first award for PLAYING HOOKIE. Later that year, several of her quilts were featured in a local art gallery for an exhibition called "When Tradition meets Imagination". After a three year period where family and business took priority, Lisa claimed her first two "Best of Shows" with HULA HIBISCUS at AQS QuiltWeek® in Des Moines, Iowa and the PA Nat'l Quilt Extravaganza in Oaks, Pennsylvania. RED VELVET and SWAN'S SONG are making their rounds and collecting ribbons on the show circuit. SWAN'S SONG garnered a first place at the Houston International Quilt Festival.

Teaching

In 2007, Lisa started teaching after producing her first book and DVD, *Feathers of a New Generation*. She has taught this as a class both at shows and in her studio. Her latest DVD *Divide and Design* was released last year and is rapidly approaching the 2,000 unit sale mark. This is also being taught at shows, in studio, and on QNNTV. *Mastering the Mini, Whole Cloth that is!* DVD was released in April 2014 to rave reviews. She has taught for the past 7 years at top quilting shows in the nation, such as MQX Quilt Festival, Home Machine Quilting Show, and Birds of a Feather.

Intelligent Quilting

In 2008, Lisa became a founding partner in Intelligent Quilting LLC, an online retail site for digital and paper patterns. She sold her interest in the business in 2011 to focus on other aspects of her career. The company has grown to over 40 designers with 1000's of pattern choices and is currently owned by Professional Longarmer Crystal Smythe.

Rulers

In 2012, the Quilter's Groove™ Rulers were introduced. The Quilter's Groove Pro Series and Pro Curve Series. Shortly after the ProEcho™ and ProCircle™ rulers were added to the line. In 2015, the ProSpine™ and ProPebble™ rulers were added and have been a huge success. All these rulers are available at lisahcalle.com.